THE BRECON JAZZ STORY

IN PHOTOGRAPHS
BY GENA DAVIES

Edited by David Moore

Adamant Band entertaining a crowd in Bulwark, 2005, photographed with a wide-angle lens. Members include, from left: Ron King, trumpet; Steve Davies, sousaphone; Jim Wood, band marshall; Geoff Palzer and Bob Davies, trombones.

THE BRECON JAZZ STORY
IN PHOTOGRAPHS
BY GENA DAVIES

Contents

Preface

It is surprising that, as the thirtieth festival approaches, little has been produced to celebrate the development of a festival as renowned internationally as Brecon Jazz. Organisers in recent years have, understandably, been more concerned about its financial survival than with recording historic achievements. Long-term enthusiasts will recall a dramatic multi-media exhibition at Brecknock Museum and Art Gallery in 1993, *The Jazz Route to Brecon*, to mark the tenth festival. Curated by Branwen Iorwerth and Jed Williams, it was designed by Graeme Galvin and funded by the Development Board for Rural Wales. There was an accompanying booklet which included an historical overview of the festival by Stuart Nicholson. To continue the celebration to the end of the first decade, the exhibition was also shown in 1994. It evolved into Brecon's Jazz Gallery which, sadly, did not survive. Intriguingly, the distinctive Brecon Fringe had evolved to such an extent by 2009 that it become the subject of its own publication by local photographer Huw Parsons.

The Brecon Jazz Story in Photographs by Gena Davies is a significant, yet personal, visual record of the festival from its formation in 1984 until the present. While it is, inevitably, selective it encompasses major concerts, legendary musicians, stroller and fringe events, busking, life in the streets and activities behind the scenes. It is a celebration of past achievements from the standpoint of a Brecon resident who has experienced the festival closely. A comprehensive history of the festival and detailed exploration of the music and musicians has yet to be compiled.

Gena Davies was brought up in Pontypridd but has lived in Brecon since 1971. As she photographed the festival, her knowledge of jazz expanded. I have known Gena's evocative and sensitive jazz photographs for many years and, in this book, I have tried to explore something of her background and how she became so passionately interested in photographing the festival. Gena herself has written a personal account of the jazz festival which, together with her photographs and accompanying commentary, provide fascinating insights.

The book would not have been possible without the encouragement and financial support of the Brecknock Art Trust. Additional funds collected in memory of the late Tony Elston, a director of the festival, as well as from the Brecknock Society and Museum Friends have made a significant contribution. A vital member of the project has been Sue Hiley Harris, who is responsible for the considerable tasks of both design and technical preparation for publication. Jean Hosie has provided valuable information about the formation of the festival and has advised on a draft of the text. I am also grateful for the enthusiastic support of Pablo Janczur, current director of Brecon Jazz with Orchard Media and Events Group. He is well aware of the festival's rich heritage.

David Moore
Crooked Window, Brecon
June 2013

Opposite: Jazz vocalist and critic George Melly at the first Brecon Jazz in 1984.
He owned a house at Scethrog, near Brecon, from where he would fish in the River Usk.
'It was decided to hold the festival on the only weekend that he was available.
Here he is wearing stickers supporting the miners' strike.'

Gena Davies: A Journey into Jazz Photography
David Moore

Gena Davies has lived in the historic Welsh market town of Brecon since 1971. Passionately interested in drawing from an early age, she developed a strong interest in photography later in life. This has found expression in a remarkable record of the town's jazz festival. Founded in 1984, this international celebration of the music attracts thousands of visitors to Brecon in August each year.

Born in 1943, Gena was brought up in the south Wales industrial town of Pontypridd. She was particularly influenced by her mother, an art teacher at the local girls' grammar school. Her father, a gardener and handyman at the School of Mines, Treforest, also valued education as a means of progressing in life.

Gena was encouraged to take an interest in art and, even today, is a compulsive drawer. 'I got into trouble with a lot of the teachers in class because I was drawing rather than listening to what they were saying,' she recalls. 'I didn't enjoy school very much.' As her mother taught at the same school, Gena was transferred to Our Lady's Convent in Cardiff, travelling there each day by train.

With art her best subject, and following in her mother's footsteps, Gena attended Cardiff Art School in 1959, continuing to travel from Pontypridd. Sadly, this coincided with the illness and, in the second term, death of her father. 'I expected my time there to be a liberating experience but, instead, found the atmosphere at the art school terrifying. The older students threw their weight about to impress those in the first year. Everything I thought or did seemed to be considered stupid, ridiculous or both. I started to lose confidence. I felt confused, unhappy and began to believe that I would never fit in.' At the end of her first year, it was clear that she was not enjoying life at art school and she left, with no clear idea about what she would do next.

In the summer of 1960 she became, for a short period, a probationary reporter on *The Pontypridd Observer*, which she enjoyed. She interviewed a young rock singer called Thomas Woodward 'who was causing a sensation among all the local teenage girls.' He later became better known as Tom Jones. 'I remember describing him as 'Ponty's own Elvis' and having an earnest discussion with the sub-editor about whether I was allowed to describe him as sexy!' Her career in journalism was frustrated, however, when the newspaper acquired new owners and there were staff cuts. 'Since I was still on probation,' she recalls sadly, 'I was the first to be dismissed.'

Gena tried other professions. She spent a year at a teacher-training college near Rugby. 'I did one teaching practice. It wasn't too successful, I gather. There was a certain problem with keeping discipline.' Librarianship was suggested and, for six months, she became a library assistant at Hereford City Library. 'I began to realise why Hereford still had two chained libraries; people weren't always that good at bringing books back.'

When her grandmother became ill, Gena returned to Windsor Road, Pontypridd. Her close-knit family lived in the surrounding streets and she helped to care for her grandmother until she died.

In the late 1960s Gena, responding to a call for Welsh applicants, was auditioned for the radio quiz game *Brain of Britain*. 'I rather liked the idea,' she admits, 'of showing off and competing with other people.' The programme was recorded in London and she won the first round. 'Somehow or other, I found myself in the final and was the runner-up. That helped to bolster my self-confidence. I was suddenly a local celebrity, even if I did not have the same star-rating as Tom Jones.'

Gena had just become a junior assistant librarian at Pontypridd Public Library, a job title which, she readily admits, 'accurately described my place in the library's pecking order.' There was mounting resentment at her quiz show success. 'The fact that people were asking me questions was getting up the qualified librarian's nose a bit. Staff decided that I needed to be put in my place.' Curiously, she also kept getting into trouble for reading books. 'Reading on duty: definitely not! From what I gather, in libraries, books are to be sorted, stamped, catalogued, repaired and shelved but never read. I often surrendered to the temptation to peep inside the covers. This was an unforgivable sin.'

Gena endured the library for about three years but parted company with it at the end of the 1960s. 'I became depressed and had difficulty concentrating on my work. I asked for help from the doctor but the drug I was prescribed made me so sleepy that I made more mistakes than ever, which made the tension between me and the staff even worse. Eventually, I could no longer cope with the stress and resigned.'

Shortly after Gena left the library, her mother retired from teaching and they decided to move away from Pontypridd. Gena had learned to drive and they used to explore the countryside. 'Brecon was a place we visited frequently. We liked the atmosphere of the country market town which was very different from that of Pontypridd although it was only about an hour's drive away.' They moved into a bungalow on a new estate on the northern side of Brecon in 1971. 'It was like another world. It had an entirely different atmosphere. I have lived in Brecon since then and have been very happy here.'

In 1975 Gena made another national quiz show appearance. This time it was in *Mastermind*, then a relatively new television programme. Answering questions about horses - a familiar subject as she had ridden ponies from an early age - she made it to the second round for the best runners-up.

Gena started to sketch again, mainly watercolour landscapes. 'I began,' she reflects, 'to regain the confidence I had lost at art school'. Parking in roadside gateways, she would often be interrupted by someone wishing to pass through. She took photographs so that, if she had to move or if the weather deteriorated, she would be able to use them to finish the sketch.

This led to an interest in photography for its own sake: 'I found the inhibitions which hindered my painting did not seem to apply to this.' At first she used an ordinary compact camera but was later able to buy a single-lens reflex camera. 'I was left a bit of money and I thought I'd acquire a really good camera. I bought this Yashica FX-D, all the works, the latest thing, but I was getting far worse results with it than with my old camera.'

She researched photography in the library and joined Brecon Camera Club. The proprietor of a local photography shop provided advice. Having learned about black and white photography, she discovered that she preferred it to working in colour. 'The results returned from the laboratories were often disappointing,' she discovered. 'I decided I must try home processing and found it challenging but rewarding.'

At first, Gena photographed landscapes. 'I had ambitions', she muses, 'to be the Ansel Adams of Brecon Beacons National Park.' She entered camera club competitions and exhibited.

'I did a bit of work,' she recalls, 'for people who wanted photographs for the local paper.' This included local carnivals and shows. Nevertheless, 'they didn't publish that many of my photographs. In those days it was still half-tone blocks in *The Brecon & Radnor Express*.' Press work helped her to experiment. 'I could do the photographs, go home, develop the film, let it dry and then do the prints, say, on Sunday and have it ready by Monday.' She also provided publicity material for Brecknock Little Theatre.

It was with complete disbelief that Gena heard, in 1984, about plans for a jazz festival in Brecon. 'I just couldn't believe that it was serious. It didn't fit in with what I knew of Brecon. I decided to walk into town to see what was going on. I took my camera with me. Free entertainment was promised and this suggested plenty of opportunities for photography.'

When, shortly after the first festival, the organisers asked for photographs for publicity purposes, Gena submitted prints. These were exhibited in Brecon Library. 'Not that many others were taking pictures,' she recalls. The festival organisers kept asking her for images. 'The dustbin photographs got taken for publicity for *Keep Wales Tidy* at later festivals'.

After several years, Gena had not only learned a great deal about jazz but was becoming interested in the festival as a photographic subject. 'That's why I kept on taking photographs. I was learning a bit technically, too. When it started, I didn't know whether I liked jazz or not although I liked a live performance.'

She got to know some of the festival organisers including the committee chair, Liz Elston. 'When they brought in the press pass I was a bit worried but Liz obtained one for me and, then, I could keep on saying: 'Well, I had one last year'.

At first, Gena used flash for indoor and low-light work but, as some musicians objected to this, she started to experiment with uprated film. This involved setting the camera for a higher film speed than was the case. The underexposed result needed to be developed for longer, affecting contrast, graininess and resolution. 'I had a large number of failures at first but persisted, especially when I saw how using this technique increased the atmosphere of the photographs I took.' She would, eventually, acquire a second single-lens reflex camera, a Contax 139, enabling her to use both colour and black and white film with one adjusted for uprated film.

Some of her photographs, including one of George Melly, were bought for Brecknock Museum and Art Gallery. 'Talking to other photographers,' she reveals, 'I realised that the photographs which I had already taken were a valuable historical record.'

After her mother died in 1992, Gena tried to get back into employment. 'I went through all the hoops. Got extra qualifications in typing and word processing. Learned about computers. Did all the right things. But they weren't interested in people my age.' She worked for a short period in a factory and, later, a supermarket, but she found them both a dispiriting experience.

Gena had, early in the festival, become a voluntary steward and she was usually allocated to the venue in the Viaduct Car Park. From 1997, when Theatr Brycheiniog was built, until 2007 she was a voluntary theatre steward. During the festival she was restricted to stewarding at the theatre only and this limited opportunities to take photographs elsewhere. 'I got to know the theatre pretty well. You knew what the stage looked like from different angles including ones that the professional photographers didn't use, such as from the balcony.' Eventually, however, it was decided that she would no longer be permitted to take photographs while, at the same time, working as a steward. This allowed her more freedom to take photographs at other venues.

Gena learned a lot from talking to professional photographers. 'That was another reason why I got into trouble at the theatre because I was talking to the other photographers about their equipment and who they were working for. I'm not quite sure what they thought of me, a sort of amateur. There were some real specialists. Some of them said they liked my photographs which had been on display in the museum.' They used the first digital cameras that Gena had encountered.

She acquired a Canon EOS 300D and another compact digital camera. 'The technical skills in low-light photography that I had taught myself over the years were obsolete in a world of computers and Photoshop. It took time to adjust to the new equipment, though I was happy to say goodbye to the days of labouring in the darkroom, going through packets of paper while trying to produce the perfect print.'

Gena recalls her exhibition in 2008 at St Mary's Church to mark the festival's twenty-fifth anniversary. 'The president that year was Richard Livsey, for whom I had worked for while when he was campaigning to be re-elected as Brecon and Radnor's Member of Parliament. With his encouragement, I approached the festival committee for support. Some images were also reproduced in the festival programme alongside the work of professional jazz photographers.'

For Gena, Brecon Jazz photography has became an end in itself. Her considerable archive is, undeniably, a significant record of the festival. She does not know of anyone else who has taken photographs of it continually since 1984. Emphatically, she is not a professional jazz photographer. 'I couldn't really afford to start doing that. I'm an amateur; doing it for love, you could say.' For most of the time she photographs landscapes although, in the past, she has taken musicians at the local jazz club. Recently, too, she has been studying stone-carving with sculptor Richard Renshaw. Nevertheless, she has created a remarkable legacy of jazz photographs for Brecon, the festival, its supporters and jazz enthusiasts worldwide.

Opposite: Adamant Band being followed by the public up Castle Street, 1984.
The leading musicians are, from left: Jim Wood, sousaphone; Geoff Palzer and Mike Harries, trombones.

A temporary café on the zebra crossing at the eastern end of Bulwark, 1984.

Adamant Band approaching the George Hotel with Krukke outside, 1984.

Opposite: Local cheer-leaders leading Adamant Band in High Street (top) and with Krukke, or Breda Carnival Band, outside the Clarence in Watton (below), 1984.

Brecon Jazz: A Personal View
Gena Davies

The news that Brecon was going to have a jazz festival in August 1984 was received with bewildered disbelief by most local people. It seemed extremely unlikely. Brecon is a small country town in central Wales, a part of Britain where sheep outnumber people. Agricultural shows, sheepdog trials and the occasional carnival and village fête were the normal summer entertainments. These were reported in minute detail by the local newspaper to lighten up the main news. There were equally detailed accounts of local funerals. Jazz festivals, it was believed, happened in more sophisticated places. It was conceded, reluctantly in some cases, that this one would be interesting and different.

The idea of a jazz festival in Brecon might have seemed improbable but it had, in fact, been nearly a year in preparation. It was the consequence of the failure of an earlier plan of the organisers, Brycheiniog Association for the Arts, to buy the disused Bethel Chapel for conversion into an arts centre. During a meeting to discuss alternative projects, Tony Constantinescu, who had recently visited Breda Jazz Festival in the Netherlands, suggested that Brecon would be suitable for a similar event. Another member, Liz Elston, had regularly attended jazz clubs when living in London as an art student. She liked the idea and, together, they convinced other committee members that it was feasible. A group, including Jean Hosie and John Morgan, was set up to explore the idea. The support of the town and borough councils was obtained through councillors Geoff Harding and Tony Elston. The police were amenable to the suggestion of closing streets for the event. The Welsh Jazz Society was asked for help. Jed Williams, its director, was enthusiastic and offered his full support.

George Melly, jazz vocalist and critic, lived near Brecon at Scethrog. The committee decided to ask for his support. He agreed, although he complained later that jazz, his 'jealous mistress' for forty years, had found her way along the A40 to his secret retreat where he indulged his other love, trout fishing.

The next problem to be dealt with was that of funding. This was not so much limited as non-existent. An unsolicited donation from Brecknock Tourist Association primed the pump. The committee set about raising funds from local businesses. Eventually, enough money was raised to match-fund a grant application to South East Wales Arts Association. This was obtained and the event went ahead on the only weekend that George Melly was available, the third weekend of August.

When the day of the festival arrived, a large crowd gathered in the town centre. The majority had little idea what to expect or even if they would enjoy the experience. Everyone, however, appreciated the absence of traffic. While some stood in small groups, chatting in what was normally the middle of the busy High Street, others investigated stalls which charities had set up to raise money and provide information about their activities. Some pubs and cafés had set out chairs and tables on the pavement and road, giving High Street and Bulwark an unfamiliar, yet attractive, continental appearance. These soon attracted customers. A bandstand had been placed in Bulwark outside the east end of St Mary's Church and, as the hands of the clock moved closer to the time of the official opening, the crowd grew bigger. At eleven o'clock Breda Carnival Jazz Band, or Krukke, and Adamant, a New Orleans-style band from Cardiff, marched in accompanied by cheer-leaders and local ladies dancing the Charleston. Brecon's first jazz festival had begun.

For the next two days every corner of Brecon swung to the sound of jazz. Krukke and Adamant paraded around town. At the Boar's Head, beside the Usk, veteran saxophonist Benny Waters and pianist Red Richards entertained an appreciative audience. The Market Hall roof was raised to the height of the Beacons by George Melly and John Chilton's Feetwarmers. The Saline Big Band, from Brecon's American twin town, was also in the programme. Bulwark bandstand was occupied by a succession of bands and soloists including the French Hot Antic Jazz Band, the Memphis Seven - who were more familiar with the Towy than the Mississippi - and the Hot Cotton Jazz Band, which really did come from Memphis, Tennessee. At the Cathedral the Adamant Band made 'a joyful noise unto the Lord' for the Sunday morning festival service. By the afternoon people were dancing in the street. Slim Gaillard enthusiastically prophesied that Brecon Jazz would have a great future. This was greeted by equally enthusiastic cheers from his audience.

Shortly after the festival a feature, submitted by local journalist Tony Heath, appeared on the front page of *The Guardian*. It did not make the front page of *The Brecon and Radnor Express* because, at the time, this showed only advertisements. The newspaper did, however, give the event a whole page report with many public comments that it was what the town needed. Brecon's first jazz festival was, undoubtedly, a popular success. The organisers, Brycheiniog Association for the Arts and the Welsh Jazz Society, had every reason to feel pleased with themselves. They did not, however, relax and enjoy a well-deserved break. Planning for the next festival began before the last notes of the first had ended.

In the early summer of 1985 Brecon was the centre of a closely-fought parliamentary by-election. Receiving nationwide television coverage, the media sent cameras and reporters to cover the live announcement of the result. This gave the second jazz festival a great deal of free publicity. Journalists invariably mentioned it when describing the kind of town that Brecon was, although they usually sounded amazed that such an event had occurred in a place considered to be a remote rural area. The election count was held at the Guildhall on the morning after polling day. Banners advertising the festival appeared prominently in the broadcasts. The winning candidate, Richard Livsey, enjoyed jazz and would, later, become the festival's chairman and president.

The festival committee had to live up to the success of the first event. Jed Williams, the director of music, invited back some of the previous year's favourite performers such as Krukke, Adamant Band, Benny Waters and Slim Gaillard. He also brought in new guests including Stan Tracey, Jan Garbarek, for his first Welsh appearance, and adventurous young musicians such as Iain Ballamy and Django Bates. There were more ticketed concerts, there was more free music and sound amplification was improved.

The large tensile street canopies first appeared in 1985. These multicoloured canvas polygons were stretched across Bulwark and High Street. They sheltered people in the street and musicians on the bandstands, providing protection from the sun, if they were lucky, or from rain, if the Welsh weather behaved in a more traditional way. They soon became a feature of the festival although, for a photographer, sunlight filtered through canvas gave the musicians rather odd colours.

The 1985 festival was the subject of a series of television programmes although, as they were made by the Welsh language television channel S4C and only shown on that channel, the audience was restricted. The following year, however, the festival was covered more widely by other channels. It appeared on the 1986 British Petroleum calendar for August and received a merit award from the British Tourist Board, the only one in Wales that year. Two years later, it was granted an award from the National Music Council for Best Exclusively Music Festival of 1987.

The dramatic growth of the festival brought fresh challenges. The problem of litter was tackled with bins, painted by local schools, and teams of volunteer litter-pickers recruited from the younger members of the Cathedral choir, army cadets and Friends of the Earth. Even the statue of the Duke of Wellington in Bulwark was dressed up to advertise the anti-litter message.

Some problems proved more difficult to deal with than litter. The first festival had been almost trouble free. The police commented that it had been quieter than a normal summer weekend. As word of the festival spread and more people came along, it became clear that a few of them had not only come to enjoy the music. Having bulk-bought cheap alcoholic drinks from supermarkets away from Brecon, they sat around in groups consuming it until they were extremely drunk. Many people found their behaviour offensive. *The Brecon and Radnor Express* published letters complaining about 'drunken rowdies' and the festival was blamed for attracting them. Access to official music venues was controlled by stewards and, consequently, they had much less trouble as disruptive people could be refused entry or expelled.

Nevertheless, five years after the first event, Brecon had become famous as the home of a major jazz festival attracting international stars. Jed Williams's music policy had been central to this success. He had encouraged a broad range of bands, styles and prices. Alongside the concerts, free music took place in the street. Adamant and Krukke formed the basis of this but they were, later, joined by bands such as Samba Galêz - which originally appeared as Cardiff School of Samba - and Wonderbrass.

Bandstands were added as the festival grew. These were at the Bishop's Garden, below the Cathedral, and in car parks off Captain's Walk and Struet, the latter on the site of a former viaduct. Many bands which had, formerly, played at the free music venues in the town centre were moved to these sites. Outdoor venues had seating, toilets and even shelter. Both the Bishop's Garden and the Viaduct Car Park were set on slopes with stages at the downhill end. This gave everyone a good view of the stage, which was not the case in the town centre, and these sites soon became very popular. Sitting on the grass in the Bishop's Garden on a sunny afternoon while listening to the band was a very enjoyable experience.

Opposite: Canopies, designed by Peter Jones and sponsored by Ford Motor Company, stretched over High Street, 1985.
'This was the first time they were used. They were a very good idea, especially if the weather was a bit dodgy.'
Right: Nathan Davis from the United States playing a soprano saxophone at the new stroller venue in the Bishop's Garden, 1986.

Slim Lightfoot and the Backbones, part of the festival's street music programme, by the Duke of Wellington's statue, Bulwark, 2008: Orlando Shearer, double bass; Chicken-King Schultz, drums; Slim Lightfoot, vocals and electric guitar.

At the beginning, there were two types of ticket. One was for individual concerts in the Guildhall and Market Hall. The other, a 'crawler' ticket, allowed entry to pubs, hotels, clubs and other music venues which charged admission. In 1984 this also covered a Humphrey Lyttleton concert in the Market Hall and provided concessions at some evening concerts.

In 1986 the 'crawler' became the 'stroller' ticket, providing access to specific stroller venues. Later, it became possible to buy strollers for either the whole weekend or for individual days. A much cheaper 'open-air' ticket was added in 1988 providing admittance to outside venues only. Children under fourteen, who were accompanied by an adult, were admitted free and so it was, sometimes, billed as a 'family' ticket.

Conditions listening to stroller events at indoor venues were similar to those at ticketed concerts although open-air venues were much more informal. Access to indoor events was limited by health and safety restrictions on numbers and that was determined by the size of the venue. People might be turned away from the Castle Hotel ballroom because of overcrowding but outdoor sites, such as Captain's Walk and the Bishop's Garden, always had plenty of space. The stroller ticket provided access to a wide variety of bands and encouraged people to experiment with different kinds of jazz. If you liked the sound, it was possible to walk into an event and, if you did not, you could wander away unobtrusively. Many musicians on the stroller programme, such as Mike Harries or Keith and Marcia Pendlebury, came every year and had a dedicated following.

The ticketed concerts increased in number from four, at the original festival, to twenty-five ten years later. They did not just attract the top British musicians but also all-time international jazz greats including Gerry Mulligan in 1991, Lionel Hampton, Wynton Marsalis and Stephane Grappelli in 1993, George Shearing in 1994 and Illinois Jacquet in 1996. Major sponsorship was attracted from sources such as British Airways and the Pharos Group.

The artistic director Jed Williams's sudden death at the age of fifty-one in November 2003 was a sad loss for the festival. It was remarked later that, as someone who loved jazz, he ran the festival with the intention of sharing his passion for the music with as many people as possible. Andy Eagle was executive director until 2005 with Jim Smith as director of music and, then, director until 2008. The Welsh Assembly Government, with the enthusiastic support of First Minister Rhodri Morgan, provided financial security. HSBC sponsored the festival for the last three years of this period.

The committee kept to the successful formula of free street music, stroller venues and ticketed concerts for established stars. Complaints about rowdiness, however, led to the police putting extra restrictions on street music and imposing charges for policing the event. The festival's organisers responded by cutting back the street music. They dismissed, in 2004, the Dutch Krukke band which had been visiting the festival since 1984, even acquiring Brecon members. This seemed hard as it had been called upon during previous festivals to entertain unruly crowds late into the evening.

The festival's silver jubilee in 2008 promised a star-studded programme with even more events than usual. The weather did not co-operate. It rained heavily on both Saturday and Sunday and the result was disastrous. Sales of tickets for outdoor events were extremely low. Courtney Pine asked his audience to jump for joy during his concert in the Watton Marquee. Ankle-deep in mud, they could only respond with a syncopated squelch. Poor ticket sales contributed to the bankruptcy of the festival and many wondered if it was finally over.

Hay Festival, renowned for managing successful literary events worldwide and to budget, was selected by the Arts Council of Wales to run the festival from 2009 for three years. Its director Peter Florence appointed Sarah Dennehy as jazz programme director. Taking on the festival at short notice, it sought to reduce costs and removed most free music and the stroller and outdoor concerts from the programme. The festival consisted, largely, of ticketed concerts. Acker Bilk, Hugh Masekela and Allen Toussaint all performed during this period. A street parade, however, was introduced and took place in the first two years.

Despite this, local concern about the festival was now less about its rowdiness than that it no longer included many events which families with small incomes could enjoy. A festival fringe had existed in some form since 1984. The Plough Chapel's annual flower festival dated from the first jazz festival and there was a well-established programme of events in local pubs, clubs, art galleries, shops and cafés. These included a wide-range of music and most of the local pop and folk groups. It became more organised, from 2006, as Brecon Fringe Festival, which adapted and grew in response to changes in Brecon Jazz policy. The fringe booked some of the favourite musicians from the old stroller programme including Adamant Band which, controversially, was dropped from the official festival in 2010.

In 2011 Hay Festival continued the previous year's trend of moving many concerts away from the town centre to the grounds of Christ College. This included not booking Theatr Brycheiniog. It appeared to be organising the jazz festival on similar lines to the Hay Festival itself, where all the events took place in marquees on the outskirts of town. Partly for financial reasons, however, Hay Festival did not continue to run the festival after 2011.

Following discussions with a local stakeholder group and Powys County Council, the Arts Council for Wales co-ordinated the selection of a new operator. Orchard Media and Events Group, based in Cardiff, were contracted for the challenging task of arranging the festival from 2012. With little time to prepare, directors Pablo Janczur and Tim Powell organised a successful festival which included Dionne Warwick, Roy Ayres and Stan Tracey in the programme.

Brecon Jazz has become an important part of the cultural life of the town and is celebrated throughout the jazz world. Despite recent financial difficulties, the festival endures and is something of which Wales can, justifiably, be proud.

Slim Gaillard, who prophesied that Brecon Jazz would have a great future, playing piano outside St Mary's Church in Bulwark with Lionel Davies on bass, 1984 (above). Gaillard (also shown opposite) was described in the programme as a 'remarkable guitarist, dancer, pianist, drummer, composer, inventor of language, singer and improviser supreme.'

'Pandy Jones, a local man (shown above with Gaillard), was clowning around. He got very hot and took off his latex mask to the horror of a small child, who then said to Slim: "You're not going to take your face off, are you?"'

Above: Benny Waters, an American saxophonist who had recorded with King Oliver and was living in Paris. He was playing at the Boar's Head accompanied by Red Richards, 1984.

Opposite: New York stride pianist Red Richards in Bulwark, 1984.

An appreciative audience dancing outside St Mary's Church, Bulwark, 1984 (above) to West Midland's pianist Tommy Burton with Gordon Whitworth on trumpet. John Gibbon from Abergavenny was playing drums (opposite). Burton is also shown from behind the stage (opposite, top) beneath a small tensile canopy which was installed on the festival's second day by local artist Peter Jones. This was the inspiration for the extensive street canopies which he designed for the 1985 festival.

Cornet player Warren Vaché (opposite) playing with the traditional jazz Hot Cotton Band from Memphis, Tennessee,
outside St Mary's Church, 1984 (above). Shown in the front line are, from left: Clive Collins, trombonist; Warren Vaché;
George 'Doc' Ryan, leader and cornet player; Bob Baker, clarinettist.
*'Bulwark bandstand was occupied by a succession of bands and soloists. They were still selling LPs and not CDs then.
I made a mistake with Warren Vaché. One arm was in a sling but, without realising, I did not include it in the photograph.*

Above: Canopies surrounding the statue of the Duke of Wellington, Bulwark,1986.
'He wore a different hat every year.'

Opposite: The festival opening in Bulwark, 1985.
'Krukke are on the platform getting ready to play. Richard Livsey, a Liberal elected to the constituency in a notable by-election a few months earlier, opened the festival. He later became involved in running it.'

American guitar player Al Casey with south Wales musicians, bass player Dave Greensmith (above) and pianist Russ Jones (left) outside St Mary's Church, Bulwark, 1985. Earlier in his career, Casey played with Fats Waller. Greensmith was a co-founder of the Welsh Jazz Society.

Opposite: Fapy Lafertin, a guitarist from Belgium who played in the gypsy tradition of Django Reinhardt, Bulwark, 1985.

Above: Listening to music performed on a canal barge, 1986.
The site would, by 1997, be developed into a canal basin adjacent to the new Theatr Brycheiniog.
'This was one of the fringe events.'

Opposite: John Marsden, principal of Coleg Hywel Harris, chair of the festival's publicity committee and a Rotarian, selling hats in the High Street to raise funds for local charities, 1986.

In Bishop Williamson Garden, 1986, saxophonist Iain Ballamy (left) performing with his quartet including pianist Django Bates and drummer Steve Arguelles (above).

'I don't remember many other people taking photographs in the early years. I was asked to take photographs by the festival organisers for publicity.'

The Bishop's Garden looking towards Struet, 1986.
'This venue opened for the first time that year. The Iain Ballamy Quartet was playing.'

In Captain's Walk,
another new venue
for 1986, trumpeter
Digby Fairweather
(opposite) performs
with pianist Keith
Pendlebury and bass
player Dave
Greensmith (right).

*'Keith Pendlebury
came every year
with his wife,
Marcia. He was
never really
separated from
that beer mug.
The hat usually
ended up being
thrown into the
crowd at the end
of the session.
I always tried to
take it in the air but
I never got it right.'*

Above: South African Dudu Pukwana on soprano saxophone in the Market Hall, 1986, where he performed with his band Zila. He had also played in the first festival.

Opposite: Scottish trombonist George Chisholm sharing a moment with his audience in the Market Hall, 1986.

Keeping Brecon tidy during the early festivals, 1984-85: The Duke of Wellington's statue, Bulwark, promoting *Keep Wales Tidy* (above); carrying a decorated oil drum bin out of Mount Street Junior School (right, top); Liz Elston, chair of Brecon Jazz, collecting bins from St Joseph's Catholic School (right, below).

'There had been complaints about litter so they asked schools if they could paint old oil drums as litter bins. I believe Elstons supplied them.'

Opposite: Young volunteers collecting litter, 1987.

'The army cadets, the Cathedral choir and the local branch of Friends of the Earth did most of it.'

Humphrey Lyttleton (opposite), who had performed with his band at the first festival, with pianist Stan Greig (left) and vocalist Helen Shapiro (above) at the Market Hall, 1987. Lyttleton was president of the Welsh Jazz Society

'There were more photographers around, it was more crowded and they were beginning to have press passes. It was a bit less fun.'

Left: A moment of relaxation, 1987.
'Keep it cool.'

Below: The Heavy Quartet, from Cardiff, playing on a lorry bandstand in High Street, 1987. They were described in the programme as 'strolling players', along with Krukke and Adamant.

'It was getting a bit rougher, especially in the evenings. A lot of people came along with drinks from out-of-town supermarkets. It was beginning to change the character of the festival.'

Opposite: Scottish guitarist Martin Taylor at the Castle Hotel, 1988.

'This was one of my early experiments in uprated film for low-light photography without flash. I very rarely got good photographs in the Castle Hotel ballroom as they often placed musicians in front of the big window.'

Australian trumpeter Bob Barnard (opposite, top) playing
with the Harlem Blues and Jazz Band from the United States
in the Market Hall, 1988, with vocalist Laurel Watson (above),
guitarist Al Casey and bass player John Williams (opposite,
right), tenor saxophonist George Kelly (opposite, left) and
trombonist James Buxton, a veteran of famous big bands (right).
'This was the last time I used flash in the Market Hall.'

Clarinettist Wyn Lodwick (above) playing at the new British Gas Wales Bandstand in the Viaduct Car Park, 1988.
This venue, seen opposite in 1989, was used with different sponsors until 2003. It is now on the route of the inner ring road, Heol Gouesnou.

'A Welsh speaker from Llanelli, he used to present jazz programmes on S4C and claimed to have introduced jazz to the National Eisteddfod. The bandstand was where people more interested in traditional jazz used to end up. It had a natural slope so you could see from practically anywhere.'

Above: Adamant Band at the Sunday morning jazz service in the Cathedral, 1989. This has been a regular and distinctive feature of the festival since the beginning.

'This was an awkward moment. I didn't intend to go to the service. I was passing and the verger, said: "Why don't you come in and take some photos. I'll get you a good position." As he was taking me to my seat, the band marched in. I was trying to go up the central aisle with the band just behind me. Not exactly the most unobtrusive entrance. I was left next to the bishop's chair which was, of course, occupied by the bishop.'

Opposite: Krukke from Breda in the Netherlands, High Street, 1989.

'They were considered, by that time, to be practically part of the town and local trumpeter David Jones even played with them. They used to stay at the St David's Ursuline Convent School and, sometimes when not playing, they stood on the fire escape and just listened.'

Cornet player Rod Mason (above), then living in Germany, was performing with his Hot Five together with special guest Beryl Bryden on washboard (opposite) as part of the stroller programme at the British Gas Bandstand in the Viaduct Car Park, 1990.

Vocalists (left) and front-man Ondřej Havelka (opposite) with the Original Prague Syncopated Orchestra at the Market Hall, 1990.

'A nineteen-twenties and thirties style orchestra complete with costumes and microphone, which nearly gave the sound men a heart attack. Some people felt it was carrying authenticity a bit far. Things were a little confused as, due to transport problems, they arrived a bit late. Weluwe, a Dutch family band, entertained the audience until they arrived.'

Opposite: Krukke
in Lion Street, 1991,
with accordianists
Foppe Mollema (left)
and Huub Grosfeld (right).

Right: American
bop-influenced pianist
Kirk Lightsey outside the
Blue Boar (now the Rugby
Club) on the stroller
programme, Watton, 1991.

Marcia and Keith Pendlebury at the Viaduct Car Park, 1991

'They were always on the stroller ticket and came every year until Keith died in 2002. They had a strong following. Marcia kept coming, sometimes for fringe events.'

American musicians who played together at the Market Hall, 1991, included pianist Dave McKenna (left), guitarist Howard Alden (opposite, left), clarinettist Kenny Davern (opposite, right) and trumpeter Ruby Braff (below). They were joined by saxophonist Scott Hamilton, bass player Frank Tate and drummer Jake Hanna.

Photographers and a television camera team at Gerry Mulligan's Market Hall concert, 1991 (above). The American baritone saxophonist, composer and arranger was playing with his quartet (opposite). The tailor-made stage canopies by Peter Jones and Lynne Dickens, at this and other venues, were introduced in 1986.

'They had a railway track for the television camera to parade up and down in front of the stage. The photographers, who everyone complained about, stood discreetly on the side. The stewards were pretty easy-going in those days as long as you didn't actually get on the stage and interrupt the band. Most of the stewards and photographers knew each other.'

Above: Harry 'Sweets' Edison, 1993, playing in the Market Hall with the Golden Men of Jazz.
He had been an important soloist with the Count Basie Orchestra.

Opposite: Violinist Stephane Grappelli making a sound check in the Market Hall, 1993.
'This was taken using a steward's pass before the public were allowed into the hall. I stood on a chair to be on the same level as the stage. Using a long lens you could get in close without disturbing anyone. It was one of the best concerts I remember. I think 1993 was the best year.'

Lionel Hampton on drums (above) and vibraphone (opposite, top left) during his concert in the Market Hall with the Golden Men of Jazz, which included trumpeter Clark Terry (opposite, bottom left) and saxophonist James Moody (opposite, right), 1993. Harry 'Sweets' Edison, who played with them, is shown on page 61.

'Before the show, we photographers reckoned that Lionel Hampton would only do a couple of items, because he was so old, and would leave the rest to other members of the band but he played, more or less, non-stop.'

New Orleans
trumpet player
Wynton Marsalis
in the Market
Hall, 1993.

Between gigs at Pharos Bandstand, the Viaduct
Car Park, 1994: a guest solo on balloon saxophone
(right) and taking refreshment (below).

Above: Pianist George Shearing who was accompanied by bass player Neil Swainson for a seventy-fifth birthday concert in the Market Hall, 1994.

Opposite: Alto saxophonist, composer and arranger Benny Carter, who played with Paris-based Saxomania and Warren Vaché in the Market Hall, 1994.

Above and opposite: Cleo Laine and John Dankworth who appeared
with the Dankworth Generation Big Band in the Market Hall, 1995.

Above: West Coast blues pianist, singer and composer Charles Brown in the Market Hall, 1996.
'The trouble with pianists is that there is so much piano and so little pianist. The piano keeps getting in the way!'
Opposite: Betty Carter, an American singer known for her improvisational technique, at Christ College Memorial Hall, 1996.

Members of the Tom Harrell
Sextet at Christ College
Memorial Hall, 1996:
Steve Turré, trombonist
(opposite, top); Billy Hart,
drummer (opposite, bottom);
Tom Harrell, flugelhorn player,
composer and arranger (left);
Bob Berg, saxophonist (above).

George Melly (right)
in the Market Hall
for his seventieth
birthday concert with
regular collaborator,
trumpeter and jazz
historian John
Chilton (opposite)
and his Feetwarmers,
1996.

*'What the picture
of George Melly
doesn't show is the
colour of his coat.
It looks very
subdued but was
actually brilliant
orange.'*

Illinois Jacquet who accompanied
his big band in the Market Hall, 1996.

*'He'd been with Lionel Hampton at one
time. He was a tenor saxophone player but
was also a forties and fifties style singer.'*

Tenor saxophonist Joshua Redman (right)
with a view of his audience (below) in the
Market Hall, 1996.

Left: New Orleans
singer Lillian Boutté
at the newly-opened Theatr
Brycheiniog, 1997. With its
excellent acoustics this would
become an important venue
for the festival.

Opposite: Courtney Pine
playing both soprano and
tenor saxophones in the
Market Hall, 1997.

*'They had safety barriers
and, somehow, I ended up
on the wrong side of them.
I don't think they had any
rules about photography
because everyone was
getting up dancing.
I lost a few photographs
as I was being shaken
with the camera.'*

Above: American guitarist Russell Malone and Canadian singer and pianist Diana Krall exchange a glance at Theatr Brycheiniog, 1997.
Opposite: Alto saxophonist Bobby Watson at Theatr Brycheinog, 1997.

Clarinettist Kenny Davern and tenor saxophonist Scott Hamilton (left) at Theatr Brycheiniog with Hamilton, a favourite of Brecon audiences, applauding a solo (above), 1997.

'I was, officially, stewarding upstairs in the theatre. It was possible to get on the same level as the players.'

Opposite: Blues singer and guitarist John Hammond at Theatr Brycheiniog, 1998.

The Windjammers, a stroller event at Theatr Brycheiniog Suite, 1997: bass player Ben Hazleton with Brecon musicians drummer Bert Jones (left) and organist Mike Chappell (below).

Opposite: Krukke sousaphone player Harm Van Kasteren at the opening ceremony in Captain's Walk, 1998.

Right: New Orleans
saxophonist and
composer Branford
Marsalis listening to
other members of
his quartet in the
Market Hall, 1998.

Opposite:
Tenor saxophonist
Joe Lovano
silhouetted against
the stage floor in
Theatr Brycheiniog,
1998.

Left: A moment of reflection for soprano saxophonist Steve Lacy, who played with pianist Mal Waldron at Theatr Brycheiniog, 1999.

Above and right: Two images of pianist Brad Mehldau, who was playing with his trio, taken from opposing balconies at Theatr Brycheiniog, 1999.

Free-improvising soprano saxophonist Lol Coxhill (opposite) playing in *Merz Jam*, a Kurt Schwitters-inspired installation by sculptors Jeff Nuttall and Islwyn Watkins at Brecknock Museum and Art Gallery, 2000. Whilst the sculptors themselves are not shown, another artist, Pip Woolf, assisted by Gil Chambers, is crouching to make a continuous drawing in response to the music. Adamant trumpeter Ron King and his wife (above) take in the scene.

'I think a lot of people wondered what it was all about.'

Above: Pianist Kenny Barron, performing solo at Theatr Brycheiniog, 2000.

Opposite: Guitarist, composer and arranger Jim Hall, who played with his trio at Theatr Brycheiniog, 2000.

Right: Gospel singers
The Blind Boys of Alabama -
from left, Roscoe Robinson,
Clarence Fountain and Jimmy
Carter - leaving the stage after
their concert in the Cathedral,
2001. Fountain and Carter
were original members of the
group which was formed in
1939 at the Alabama Institute
for the Negro Blind.

Opposite: Guitarist and
singer Marty Grosz, born in
Berlin and now living in the
United States, at the Hay
Cinema Bookshop Bandstand
in the Viaduct Car Park, 2001.
*'He was the son of the artist
George Grosz and I think he
left Germany in a hurry in
1933 with his parents.'*

A performance of Stan Tracey's 1965 suite *Under Milk Wood*, inspired by the play for voices by Dylan Thomas, at Theatr Brycheiniog, 2001. Scottish tenor saxophonist Bobby Wellins (opposite) reprised his role in the original version. Actor Philip Madoc (above) was the narrator.

'They had a dark background with twinkling things that caught the light.'

Left:
New Orleans
trumpeter Leroy
Jones playing
with his quintet
at Theatr
Brycheiniog,
2001.
*'This was at
the invitation
of the artist
Valerie Ganz. He
normally plays
at Preservation
Hall, New
Orleans. She
drew him there
and asked for
him to be invited
to the festival.'*

Opposite:
Richard Galliano,
a French
accordionist of
Italian ancestry,
at Theatr
Brycheiniog,
2003.

Above: Chicago blues guitarist Buddy Guy at Usk Marquee, Christ College, 2002.
'It's easier to take musicians when they are talking to the audience. So often, when they are playing, they are concentrating and frowning or they've got their eyes shut. It doesn't photograph very well.'
Opposite: Belfast-born Van Morrison, in the Usk Marquee at Christ College, 2001.
'Spotlights may be dramatic but they can absolutely kill the picture by putting flare in all the wrong places.'

Soprano saxophonist
Andy Sheppard (left)
who played with
acoustic guitarist
Antonio Forcione
(opposite) and his trio
at Theatr Brycheiniog,
2002.

Right: Pianist
and composer
Ray Bryant,
originally from
Philadelphia, at
Theatr Brycheiniog,
2002.

Opposite:
Uri Caine, a pianist
from New York who
also plays classical
music, at Theatr
Brycheiniog, 2002.

Opposite: Nik Turner busking
in High Street, 2002.
*'He's played with a lot of other
musicians in the past including
the band Hawkwind.'*

Right: A double bass on double
yellow lines by St Mary's Church,
2002

Below: Cardiff School of Samba,
later renamed Samba Galêz,
outside the Punch Bowl in High
Street, 2002.

Krukke soprano saxophonist Ed Langer in Bethel Square sporting a plastic daffodil from his helmet (left). The band, led by Han Rijersberg on tenor saxophone, arriving at the opening ceremony in Captain's Walk (opposite, top), 2002.

'They stayed in Brecon and, sometimes, if there was trouble in the town centre, they would be called out again to play and calm things down.'

Opposite, bottom: Adamant entertaining a crowd at the canal basin. This was taken from Theatr Brycheiniog, 2002.

Left: Warren Vaché,
who has often appeared
at the festival since it
began, playing a
flugelhorn in a sextet
at Theatr Brycheiniog,
2003.

Opposite: Junior Mance,
a pianist predominantly
inspired by bebop, who
performed with his trio at
Theatr Brycheiniog,
2003.

*'This was taken just
as he was finishing a
number.'*

Animal Jack (right), the
Brindley family group from
Milford Haven, playing in
Brecknock Museum and Art
Gallery portico, 2005.
Oliver is playing bass with
Andy on saxophone and
Joelle (opposite) on accordian.

Above: Guy Barker, who was a guest of the young musician Pendulum Jazz Orchestra, in the Market Hall, 2007. This was one of Gena's first digital photographs.

Opposite: Cardiff singer and trombonist Mike Harries, a veteran of the stroller programme with the Root Doctors, in Captain's Walk, 2006. He founded the Adamant Band in 1961.

Trumpeter Humphrey Lyttleton (above and opposite), who played with his band and special guest Scott Hamilton at the Elston Concert in the Market Hall, 2007.

Alto saxophonist Sir John Dankworth and vocalist
Dame Cleo Lane at Watton Marquee, 2008.

Bass player Alec Dankworth (left), son of Dame Cleo Laine and the late Sir John Dankworth, at the Cathedral, 2011, and Jacqui Dankworth (right), his sister, singing on Christ College Stage, 2010.

Preparing, in Canal Road, for the carnival parade in the first year that the festival was organised by Hay Festival, 2009.
'The lady in the middle is Marcia Pendlebury. I knew the Pendleburys had a riding stables in north Wales but I didn't know they had horses like that. Apparently, their daughter specialises in breeding Portuguese Lucitanos.'

Included in the 2009 parade were Cardiff bands Samba Galêz, (above) seen heading towards the town centre along Watton, and Wonderbrass (below) in Rich Way.

Guitarist John Etheridge (above) and violinist Christian Garrick (opposite) in the acoustic quartet *Sweet Chorus* at the Cathedral, 2009. This was, originally, formed as a tribute to Stephane Grappelli and inspired by the Hot Club de France.

Opposite: Courtney Pine playing a bass clarinet at the Market Hall, 2009.

Right: A busker entertains the passers-by in Captain's Walk, 2009.

Below: A queue to hear Orquesta Buena Vista Social Club at the Market Hall trails down Castle Street and along Market Street, 2010. Long queues often form while musicians make sound checks.

Left: Floral displays in the Plough Chapel, Lion Street, a feature of the festival since 1984, with Brecon resident Mike Chappell playing an electronic organ, 2009.

Below: A quiet moment on the festival site at Christ College, 2011.

Opposite: Mick Costain from the Powys-based Repercussion Band playing a repique at Music on the Green, a fringe festival venue outside St Mary's Church, 2011.

Above: Norwegian avant-garde saxophonist and flautist Håkon Kornstad in the Cathedral, 2010. This appears to be his 'flutonett', a flute with a clarinet mouthpiece. He used live-looping, a technique to record and playback audio samples in real time.

Opposite: Local residents David Brockwell and Laurie Pyle perform at a fringe festival venue in the Cathedral Close, 2009.

Cuban singer Omara Portuondo (opposite) with the Orquesta Buena Vista Social Club
entertains an enthusiastic audience (above) in the Market Hall, 2010.

Above: Trumpeter Digby Fairweather, who played with his Half Dozen at the Market Hall, 2009.

Opposite: South African Hugh Masekela, who performed with his band in the Market Hall, 2010.
'He sang and played his flugelhorn as well as various other more African-looking instruments.'

Left: The Dean, Geoffrey Marshall, making a health and safety announcement before a concert in the Cathedral, 2012.

Opposite: The Dean and parade marshall Jim Wood lead Adamant Band down the aisle at the end of the jazz service in the Cathedral, 2011. They marched to the Castle Hotel (see page 137).

Above: In the Cathedral Close, Dean Geoffrey Marshall discusses details of the Adamant Band parade into town with sousaphone player Jim Wood and a police officer, 2010.

'This was when Adamant Band were still playing at the Cathedral service but not in the main festival. Adamant wanted to march to the Castle Hotel and were trying to arrange how not to collide with the official procession.'

Opposite: Adamant Band sitting outside the Castle Hotel as part of the fringe festival, 2011.

'They were just about to start. The missing one was probably in the bar.'

Above: Electric sitarist Mehoob Nadeem who played in Blues Sans Frontières at the Cathedral, 2011.

Opposite: London-based tenor saxophonist Art Themen who played with the John Etheridge Quartet in the Cathedral, 2011.

Above and right: Jamaican-born pianist and vocalist Monty Alexander, with Hassan Shakur on bass, in the Market Hall, 2011.

Opposite: Acker Bilk, with clarinet in hand, at the Market Hall, 2010.

Above: New Orleans pianist, songwriter and producer Allen Toussaint in the Big Tent at Christ College, 2011.
'His suit was definitely dazzling.'
Opposite: Funk and jazz saxophonist and singer Maceo Parker who appeared with the BBC Big Band in the Big Tent at Christ College, 2011.

Above: Listening to the group, Afternoon in Paris, at the fringe festival venue outside Pilgrims Tearooms in the Cathedral Close, 2012.

Opposite: Krukke, making their first appearance for ten years, at the Bishop's Garden, Priory Hill, as part of the fringe festival with Jacques Mol on cornet, Han Rijersberg on tenor saxophone and Ed Langer on soprano saxophone, 2012.

'The festival stopped inviting them. They said it cost too much. It wasn't just the band members but also various girl friends, then wives, then children. They were invited back to the fringe in 2012.'

Above: Pianist Stan Tracey in the Cathedral where he played music by Thelonius Monk in a quartet with saxophonist Bobby Wellins, bass player Andy Cleyndert and drummer Clark Tracey, 2012.

Opposite: French bass player Michel Benita who played in Trio Libero with saxophonist Andy Sheppard and drummer Seb Rochford at the Cathedral, 2012.

Above: Vibraphonist, vocalist and funk, soul and jazz composer Roy Ayers in the Market Hall, 2012.
Opposite: Vocalist Dionne Warwick at the Market Hall, 2012.

Tenor saxophonist
YolanDa Brown, who
played with her quartet
at Theatr Brycheiniog,
2012.

*'She is one of the few
women saxophone
players I've seen.'*

Index of Individuals and Bands in Photographs

Acknowledgements

Adamant Band trumpet player Eddie Williams, who died in 2013, attracting a crowd in High Street, 2002.

Gena Davies's photographs are not only a significant record of Brecon Jazz. They also capture moments in the performing lives of musicians who, sadly, are no longer alive. Some are among the greatest names in jazz anywhere in the world. All have provided considerable pleasure and entertainment to many people. We should like to dedicate this book to their memory.

The publishers and Gena Davies would like to acknowledge everyone who has, since its beginning, helped to make Brecon Jazz such a success. These include organisers, funders, volunteers, supporters, audiences, local people, those who visit the town to enjoy the atmosphere, the fringe, the media and, most importantly, the musicians, both local and international.

For this publication we should like to thank, in particular, Brecknock Art Trust for generous financial support. Funds collected in memory of the late Tony Elston, a director of Brecon Jazz with special responsibility for organising stewards, as well as from the Brecknock Society and Museum Friends have been of great assistance. The following have also been very generous with their time, information, advice and support: Peter Casaru · Mike Chappell · Liz Elston · Jayne Evans · Nigel Evans and Karin Mear, Brecon Fringe Festival · Henrietta Gresham, The Blind Boys of Alabama · Jean Hosie · Peter Jenkins · Bert Jones · David Jones, Krukke · Ken Jones · Ieuan Jones · Slim Lightfoot · Marcia Pendlebury · Amanda Renwick · Sam Ware, Repercussion Band · Jim Wood, Adamant Band. The festival and fringe printed programmes and back copies of *The Brecon & Radnor Express* have been a valuable source of information.

Text © Gena Davies and David Moore 2013
Images © Gena Davies
Image of Gena Davies © David Moore
Design Sue Hiley Harris

ISBN 978-0-9563602-2-9

Published in 2013 by Crooked Window   Printed in Wales by Cambrian Printers

Crooked Window
90 Struet, Brecon
Powys, Wales LD3 7LS
www.crookedwindow.co.uk